CHOCOLATE

Chocolate has many stories. You can start with Moctezuma the Second, who had a 'bank' full of millions of cacao beans – enough to make 25 million chocolate bars. Or with Daniel Peter, who wanted to make something new from chocolate, and tried mixing it with cheese. There are the great names of chocolate – like Fry, Hershey, and Cadbury, who made homes, schools, and gardens for their workers as well as factories.

And there are dark stories too – stories of the slaves who made the terrible journey across the Atlantic to work on the cacao tree plantations. And the children in West Africa who have to work on plantations there to get food to eat and who cannot go to school. Do they pick the beans that make *your* chocolate?

But the biggest story is the world's love for chocolate. And when you start to read it, you just have to have a little bit more . . .

OXFORD BOOKWORMS LIBRARY
Factfiles

Chocolate
Stage 2 (700 headwords)

Factfiles Series Editor: Christine Lindop

JANET HARDY-GOULD

Chocolate

OXFORD UNIVERSITY PRESS

OXFORD
UNIVERSITY PRESS

Great Clarendon Street, Oxford OX2 6DP

Oxford University Press is a department of the University of Oxford.
It furthers the University's objective of excellence in research, scholarship,
and education by publishing worldwide in

Oxford New York

Auckland Cape Town Dar es Salaam Hong Kong Karachi
Kuala Lumpur Madrid Melbourne Mexico City Nairobi
New Delhi Shanghai Taipei Toronto

With offices in

Argentina Austria Brazil Chile Czech Republic France Greece
Guatemala Hungary Italy Japan Poland Portugal Singapore
South Korea Switzerland Thailand Turkey Ukraine Vietnam

OXFORD and OXFORD ENGLISH are registered trade marks of
Oxford University Press in the UK and in certain other countries

© Oxford University Press 2011

The moral rights of the author have been asserted

Database right Oxford University Press (maker)

First published in 2011

10 9 8 7 6 5 4 3 2 1

No unauthorized photocopying

All rights reserved. No part of this publication may be reproduced,
stored in a retrieval system, or transmitted, in any form or by any means,
without the prior permission in writing of Oxford University Press,
or as expressly permitted by law, or under terms agreed with the appropriate
reprographics rights organization. Enquiries concerning reproduction
outside the scope of the above should be sent to the ELT Rights Department,
Oxford University Press, at the address above

You must not circulate this book in any other binding or cover
and you must impose this same condition on any acquirer

Any websites referred to in this publication are in the public domain and
their addresses are provided by Oxford University Press for information only.
Oxford University Press disclaims any responsibility for the content

ISBN: 978 0 19 478730 7

A complete recording of Chocolate is available in a CD Pack ISBN: 978 0 19 478729 1

Printed in China

Word count (main text): 6,591

For more information on the Oxford Bookworms Library,
visit www.oup.com/elt/bookworms

ACKNOWLEDGEMENTS

Map: p.3 by Peter Bull

The publishers would like to thank the following for permission to reproduce images: Alamy Images pp.0 (Chocolate
shop/Yadid Levy), 8 (Still Life with a Drinking Chocolate Set 1770 oil on canvas/The Art Gallery Collection),
13 (George Cadbury/World History Archive), 15 (Cocoa fruit pods on tree/CuboImages srl), 15 (Opening
a cacao fruit/Bon Appetit), 16 (Fermented cocoa beans being dried/Greenshoots Communications),
18 (Chocolate production/Bon Appetit), 20 (Slave auction in Virginia 1800s/North Wind Picture Archives),
21 (Fairtrade chocolate/Realimage), 26 (Chocolate assortment/Frank Chmura), 28 (Valentine's Day shop
display/Jeremy Sutton-Hibbert), 29 (Easter eggs/Mario Matassa), 32 (Chocolate cake/Julie Woodhouse f),
33 (Black Forest cherry gateau/Bon Appetit), 34 (Chocolate éclair/Keith Leighton), 35 (Churros and hot
chocolate/LOOK Die Bildagentur der Fotografen GmbH), 36 (Baking chocolate chip cookies/foodfolio);
41 (Restaurant workers eating ice cream/Mike Goldwater); Cadburys p.13 (Bourneville); Vladomir Cech
p.37 (chocolate painting); Corbis pp.27 (Heart-shaped chocolate cake/Envision), 39 (Chocolate terracotta
warriors/Grace Liang/Reuters), 39 (Model wears a chocolate hat/China Daily/Reuters); Getty Images
pp.6 (Mexican Indian Preparing Chocolate, from the Codex Tuleda, 1553 (vellum)/Mexican School/
The Bridgeman Art Library), 6 (Fol.152v The Crowning of Montezuma II (1466-1520) the Last Mexican
Emperor in 1502, 1579 (vellum)/Diego Duran/The Bridgeman Art Library); Photolibrary pp.10 (Cocoa
beans and cocoa powder/FoodCollection), 23 (Boy eating chocolate cake/Blend Images), 25 (Stack of
assorted chocolates/Robert Lawson/Fresh Food Images), 30 (Altar, Day of the Dead/Robert Harding Travel),
31 (Chocolate Christmas decorations/Meinrad Riedo/Imagebroker); Rex Features pp.21 (Production of
organic fair trade cocoa/Sipa Press), 26 (Chocolate truffles/Chris Schuster/WestEnd61); Science Photo
Library p.22 (Theobromine drug molecule/Laguna Design); The Advertising Archives p.11 (Van Houtens
Cocoa advert); TopFoto p.9 (An Eighteenth Century Chocolate house); Werner Forman Archive Ltd.
p.5 (Polychrome 'waisted' cylindrical vase/Collection: Edward H. Merrin Gallery, New York).

CONTENTS

1 The world of chocolate

Most people love the taste of chocolate. Some enjoy sweet milk chocolate and others prefer strong dark chocolate. But most chocolate lovers agree – there is no other food like it. It has a wonderful rich taste which stays in your mouth. Did you know that chocolate has more than 300 different flavours in it? It is no surprise that chocolate is now more and more popular in countries all around the world.

But what is chocolate and where did it first come from? Chocolate is made from the beans of the cacao tree. These trees first grew in the rainforests of Central and South America and people began to use the beans a very long time ago. The tree has large fruits called pods and these hold the beans inside. The scientific name for the cacao tree, *Theobroma cacao*, tells us about the wonderful food that comes from it. *Theobroma* means 'food of the gods'.

People now grow cacao trees in more than twenty different countries and not just in Central or South America. The trees need hot weather and you can find them in Brazil, Indonesia, Malaysia, and the Ivory Coast in Africa too. Farmers grow around 4 million tonnes of cacao beans a year and more than a third of this comes from the Ivory Coast.

Who eats the most chocolate in the world today? It is the people of Switzerland, who have 12.3 kilograms each every year! The Germans come next at 11.1 kilograms each, then the Belgians at 11 kilograms each, and the British at 10.2 kilograms each.

You can eat or drink chocolate in many different ways. There are big boxes of chocolates of different flavours, little chocolate bars that go in your bag or pocket, wonderful biscuits and large birthday cakes. In the summer you can eat chocolate ice cream, or on a cold winter's night you can drink hot chocolate to keep you warm.

Chocolate has also been important in books and films. Perhaps the most famous book is *Charlie and the Chocolate Factory* by Roald Dahl. It is the story of a poor boy who wins a visit to a wonderful chocolate factory. The factory belongs to the strange and exciting sweet-maker Willy Wonka. The book became two films, and in the second film Johnny Depp plays the clever but dangerous Mr Wonka. But this is not the only book about chocolate to become a film. There is *Like Water for Chocolate* from the Mexican writer Laura Esquivel, and *Chocolat* by Joanne Harris, which also became a film with Johnny Depp.

We can see that chocolate is in our stories, films and books today. But when did the story of chocolate itself really begin? We need to look back thousands of years ago for the answer.

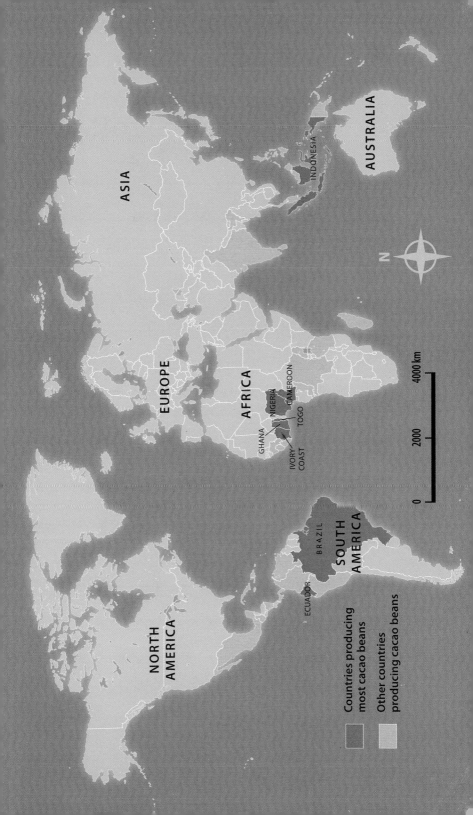

2   The first chocolate

The first people who used the pods of the cacao tree were perhaps the Olmecs three thousand years ago. The Olmecs lived deep in the rainforest in the country that is now called Mexico. People think that the Olmecs broke open the large pods of the tree to find food. But they did not use the cacao beans, they only ate the sweet white pulp around the beans. In Brazil and other places in South America people still make a drink from this soft pulp.

Since the 1970s people have also asked questions about the word 'cacao'. Where did it first come from and who used it? They have found the word 'kakawa' in the old Olmec language and they now think that 'cacao' came from there.

The earliest examples of chocolate from cacao beans come from the Maya people 1,500 years ago. These clever people lived near the same places as the Olmecs and had fine buildings and beautiful books. They were the first people to grow cacao trees and make food from the beans. We know from their pictures that chocolate was very important to them. On special days, they gave chocolate to their gods.

The Maya made a strong chocolate drink from the beans. First they took them to a warm, dark place. Then they put them in the sun to dry and later they cooked them. Next they ground them to make paste. When the paste was hard and dry they put it into water. They poured the water between two cups, from one to the other and back again, for a long time. This made a special drink with a lot of bubbles, and the Maya loved it.

They did not have sugar so they put spices in their drink for a nicer taste. At first everybody drank the chocolate, but in

A Maya pot, showing a present of white cacao beans

later times only very rich families could have it.

The Maya used special cups to drink their chocolate and people have found interesting examples of these. One cup has picture-writing for the word 'cacao' on it and there is still some chocolate inside after 1,500 years!

From around AD 1200 the Aztec people started to become more important than the Maya and they ruled over a large number of men and women. The centre of the Aztec world was the city of Tenochtitlán – today's Mexico City. Cacao trees did not grow well here because it was too dry. So the Aztecs, who loved chocolate like the Maya, began to buy cacao beans from them. In the end, these beans were very important and they became a type of money.

Pouring chocolate

Like the Maya, the Aztecs made cacao beans into a drink. They called it *chocolatl* which gave us the word 'chocolate'. They too put different spices in it and they liked it best with a very strong flavour. The Aztecs drank a lot of chocolatl and people said that the last Aztec ruler, Moctezuma the Second (1466–1520), had fifty cups of chocolate a day!

Moctezuma the Second was a very rich man and he was famous for his large 'bank' – but it was full of cacao beans, not money. One Spanish writer said that Moctezuma had 960 million beans in his bank. Today we can make around 25 million chocolate bars from that number of beans!

Moctezuma the Second

3 Chocolate comes to Europe

In the late fifteenth century, people from European countries began to explore different places in the world. In 1492, Christopher Columbus left Spain and sailed across the Atlantic to the islands of the Bahamas, northeast of the Caribbean Sea.

In the early sixteenth century, Spanish conquistadors (adventurers) started to explore Central and South America too. The conquistadors were looking for Aztec gold and silver. But they found another important thing there too – cacao beans.

The famous conquistador Hernán Cortés arrived in the Aztec city of Tenochtitlán in 1519. Moctezuma the Second welcomed the explorer with wonderful food followed by cups of chocolatl. Cortés later wrote about this drink in a letter to the King of Spain – he said that chocolate made people feel good and he described the beautiful Aztec chocolate cups.

At first, Cortés was a welcome visitor. But he soon became a dangerous enemy to Moctezuma and he fought the Aztec ruler with his large army. By 1521 Cortés and his conquistadors ruled over the Aztec people.

Cortés quickly understood that cacao beans were very important, because they were both food and money. So over the next few years Cortés started different cacao tree plantations in places that are now called Mexico, Ecuador, and Jamaica.

In 1528, Cortés went back to Spain with cacao beans for the king. He also took another important thing with him – the old Maya way to make cacao beans into a chocolate drink.

The Spanish put a secret ingredient in their chocolate – it was sugar. Chocolate was no longer the strong dark drink of the Aztecs or the Maya; it now had a nice sweet taste and it became popular all over Spain. But only rich people could drink it because it was so expensive.

At first, the Spanish drank their chocolate cold but soon they began to like it hot. They made it with bubbles – just

An eighteenth century chocolate pot and cup

like the Maya and the Aztecs. They used a small stick called a *molinillo* to make the bubbles. People made chocolate in pots with a hole in the top for the molinillo, and drank it from beautiful cups.

For nearly a hundred years, Spain kept a secret – they did not tell other countries about cacao beans and where they came from. The Spanish were the only growers of chocolate for people in Europe, and their plantations in Central America made them a lot of money.

But in 1606, an Italian traveller visited Spain and took some chocolate home with him. Then from Italy, people took chocolate to Austria and the Netherlands. News about this wonderful drink went from country to country.

In 1615, the Spanish princess Anne of Austria married King Louis the Thirteenth of France, and she took cacao beans to Paris. So the people of France began to enjoy chocolate too.

In 1657, the first chocolate house opened in London. Rich men came to these small restaurants to meet their friends and drink chocolate or coffee. The famous English writer Samuel Pepys described one of these special places in his diary in 1664: 'To a coffee house, to drink *jocolatte*, very good.'

In the seventeenth and eighteenth centuries more and more people began to drink chocolate across Europe. But when did people first start to make and eat hard chocolate? And who made the first chocolate bars?

An eighteenth century chocolate house

4   Machines and makers

By the early nineteenth century, you could find chocolate houses in towns across Europe, but not everybody liked the drinks there. Sometimes there were hard pieces of shell from the cacao beans in the hot chocolate. There is also a lot of fat, called cocoa butter, in cacao beans. This often stayed on top of the drink, and people did not enjoy that.

Around this time, people started to invent and use machines more than ever before. One Dutch inventor called Conrad Van Houten began to think about chocolate. He wanted to make a smooth drink without cocoa butter on the top. So he worked hard for many years and in 1828 he invented a machine called the cocoa press.

Cacao beans and cocoa powder

Van Houten ground cacao beans into a paste called chocolate liquor and then used his cocoa press to take out most of the cocoa butter. You can still find machines like this in chocolate factories around the world now.

Chocolate without cocoa butter is often called cocoa solids. Van Houten dried these cocoa solids and then ground them into cocoa powder. It was now smoother and much better than before and people could easily make drinks with it. We use this cocoa powder in our hot chocolate and home cooking today.

Van Houten's cocoa press was important for chocolate makers like J. S. Fry and John Cadbury in England. Later these businesses bought his wonderful machine. It worked well, but they now had a lot of cocoa butter! What could they do with it?

J. S. Fry had an answer. In 1847, he put the cocoa butter together with sugar and chocolate liquor and the world's first chocolate bar was made in Bristol, UK. Other makers like Cadbury also began to produce bars and soon boxes of smaller chocolates.

The bars were very popular, but of course people wanted to eat new types of chocolate too. So in the 1870s one inventor in Switzerland, Daniel Peter, began to put chocolate together with different things. He tried mixing chocolate with cheese but that did not work!

In 1875, Peter mixed chocolate with a special new type of sweet milk called condensed milk and he produced the world's first milk chocolate. This condensed milk was first made by Henri Nestlé in the 1860s and of course Nestlé later became a very important name in chocolate.

In 1879, another Swiss man, Rodolphe Lindt, invented a way to make chocolate even smoother. Lindt's new machine moved the chocolate around for a long time before it was made into bars. It was called a conching machine, and it produced chocolate that was beautifully smooth and easier to eat. Other chocolate makers soon began to use the machine too.

All these inventors and their machines changed the world of chocolate. In the 1890s, American Milton Hershey opened a large modern factory and began to make hundreds of thousands of milk chocolate bars. A lot of Americans could now buy a cheap Hershey Bar on the walk home from school or work.

Some of these new chocolate makers did not just want to make money or do well in business. Producers like

Cadbury, Fry, and Hershey were also very interested in the lives of their workers. They built special towns around their factories with hospitals, schools, and nice houses too.

At the end of the nineteenth century chocolate was no longer a drink for rich men and women. The new machines and factories helped working people to enjoy the taste of chocolate bars. Now you can buy and eat chocolate nearly everywhere in the world. In the next chapter we will see how chocolate is made today, beginning in a cacao tree plantation and ending in a twenty-first century chocolate factory.

Bournville – the chocolate town made by George Cadbury (right)

5   From cacao pod to chocolate bar

When we eat chocolate we often think about the wonderful flavour and we can easily forget the hard work that goes into a chocolate bar. But there is a long journey from the cacao tree plantation in Brazil or Ivory Coast to the chocolate shop near your home.

There is one surprising lesson to learn about this journey – we do many of the same things to cacao beans as the Maya and the Aztecs centuries ago. Perhaps we use machines now, but we often make chocolate in the same way as these earlier people.

The journey begins with the cacao tree and its unusual, light red flowers. These trees only grow in warm, wet rainforests. They can sometimes be difficult to grow. For example, they do not grow well if they are too cold or dry, or when it is too windy or sunny.

In the wild rainforests of Central America, the cacao trees grow under bigger trees, so on plantations people often put cacao trees under taller ones like banana trees. Plantation workers usually cut the tops of the cacao trees so they do not grow higher than eight metres.

There are different types of cacao trees. The most important type is the Forastero – over 90 per cent of the world's cacao beans come from this tree. People grow it in

Brazil and West Africa. The other type is the Criollo, which grows on plantations in Indonesia and South America. The chocolate from these beans tastes very good but the trees are more difficult to grow than the Forastero.

The cacao tree begins to have its first pods after about three years. It is very different from most other trees because its flowers and then its pods grow from the centre of the tree.

The large cacao pods are wonderful to see. At first, they are a beautiful light green. But after six months, when they are ready to open, they become very colourful. They can be bright red or orange, dark purple or deep green.

The people on the plantations take down the pods with very long sticks. Then they cut them open with big knives. Inside they find between twenty and forty cacao beans in the soft white pulp. The beans are very hard and they do not smell or taste like chocolate.

 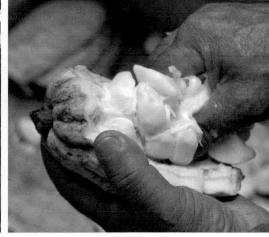

Pods on the tree, and cut open

Drying beans in the sun

The workers then usually put the beans and the pulp in large boxes with some banana leaves on the top. They leave these in the hot sun for four to seven days and some of the chemicals in the beans change.

The beans are now very different. They are no longer white or purple – they are dark brown. And very importantly they smell of wonderful chocolate!

Next, the plantation workers put the beans onto large tables. They dry the beans in the sun for ten to twenty days and move them from time to time. On larger plantations they dry them in special buildings. But the best chocolate comes from beans which stay in the sun for a long time.

The farmers then put the beans into bags of about 64 kilograms each and sell them to brokers – business people who buy and sell cacao beans for money. The brokers then sell them to the chocolate factories. But the chocolate factories do not just buy one type of bean.

Beans from different countries, or even from different plantations, taste different. In the factories, people mix together different types of bean to get chocolate with just the right taste.

At the factory, the workers first cook the beans in large machines at between 100 and 150 °C. This is very important for the flavour of the chocolate, and it usually takes about twenty minutes, but it can take longer. The beans lose their water and the shells become hard and dry.

Then the beans go into a big fast machine. This breaks open the beans and the hard shells all go to one side. After this, there are only the soft centres of the beans. The workers then put these into a big machine which grinds them into a paste. While this happens, the cocoa butter in the paste melts and the paste becomes chocolate liquor. To make chocolate bars, the workers then mix in more cocoa butter, sugar and perhaps milk.

The chocolate then goes through a special machine which grinds it again and makes it thinner. Then it is time for Lindt's famous conching machine. Some producers leave the chocolate in there for a long time – perhaps a week – and this makes the best chocolate bars.

The chocolate is now near the end of its journey, but the workers do one last thing. They make the chocolate very hot and then make it colder again. This is called tempering. The chocolate now looks very good and stays nice and smooth. They then pour it into special, square boxes and leave it until it becomes hard. At last, the chocolate bars are ready to eat!

Inside a chocolate factory

6   The darker side of chocolate

Many people around the world can sit comfortably in their homes and enjoy a nice chocolate bar. But what about the people who work on cacao plantations in some countries? Do *they* always have a comfortable life? The answer is often 'no'.

Growing cacao trees and getting the beans usually needs a lot of work. And over the years poorer people or slaves have often done these jobs. In the sixteenth century the Spanish conquistadors began to use local men and women as slaves on their cacao plantations in Central America and some Caribbean islands. These slaves had to work very long hours and they did not get any money for their work.

But many of these local slaves became ill and died from the new diseases that arrived with the conquistadors or other Europeans. And other types of plantations were beginning in both South and North America, so the plantation farmers needed large numbers of new workers. Soon people began to go to Africa to get new slaves.

Slave traders came from many countries – Portugal, Brazil, England, Scotland, France, the Netherlands, and the country that is now called the United States. They sailed to Central and West Africa, forced people onto

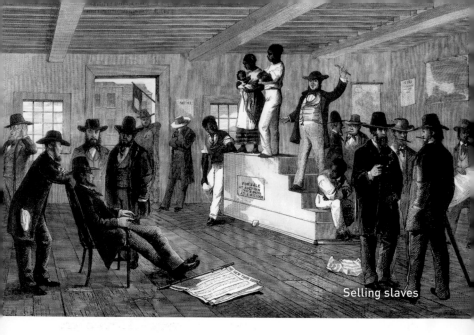

Selling slaves

their ships, and took them across the Atlantic. There they sold them to plantation farmers.

From the sixteenth to the nineteenth century between nine and twelve million Africans went across the Atlantic to work as slaves, and the slave traders made millions of dollars.

Some people think that there are slaves on cacao plantations today too. There have been stories in newspapers and on television about slaves. These news stories speak about people who take twelve- to sixteen-year-old boys from poorer African countries like Mali or Burkina Faso and sell them to plantation farmers in the Ivory Coast or Ghana.

There are also stories of child workers on cacao plantations in West Africa. Many children have to work long hours for little money. In poor families sometimes everybody needs to work, both adults and children, to get food. But the work is often hard and dangerous, and of course, these children cannot go to school.

When farmers sell their cacao beans, they usually sell them to big chocolate factories or to brokers. The brokers then sell them again for a lot of money. The farmers often do not get much for their beans, so they cannot pay their workers a lot.

In 1988, a group of people started something called Fairtrade. Fairtrade helps smaller farmers to get fair money when they sell cacao beans or other things like coffee and sugar. The farmers can then give more money to their workers for food and better houses. Only farmers who pay people fair money can sell Fairtrade cacao beans.

Fairtrade helps in other ways too. It tries to keep child workers out of the plantations and in school. In some countries cacao farmers are cutting down the rainforest to grow more cacao trees. Because of this, animals and local people that live in the rainforest are losing their homes. Fairtrade is working to try and stop this.

When you buy chocolate, you can look for the Fairtrade picture on it. A lot of smaller chocolate makers have bars made from Fairtrade cacao beans and now some bigger chocolate makers like Cadbury produce them too.

7 What is in chocolate?

A lot of people like eating chocolate and they sometimes feel good when they eat it. Why is this? For thousands of years, the Maya and the Aztecs thought that chocolate had special things in it. But nobody knew for sure. Then in 1841, a Russian man called Alexander Woskresensky found the chemical theobromine in cacao beans. Theobromine is a type of stimulant – when you eat it you can feel brighter and a little more alive.

Theobromine is not only in chocolate, you can find it in tea too. But this chemical is not always a good thing. For example, it is very bad for dogs, cats, and horses. So you must never give chocolate to these animals!

Chocolate has got another stimulant in it – caffeine. We usually find this in drinks like coffee or tea. But chocolate does not have a lot of caffeine. A small bar of dark chocolate (chocolate without milk) has only 25 per cent of the caffeine in a cup of coffee, and a bar of milk chocolate has only 10 per cent.

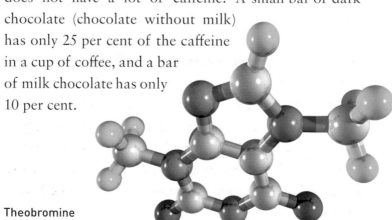

Theobromine

Some doctors think that there are some very helpful chemicals in dark chocolate too. Perhaps in the future they will be able to use these chemicals to make people well.

But of course, chocolate can also be bad for you. Many bars have a lot of sugar in them and this is not good for your teeth. Some producers also put cheap vegetable fat into their milk chocolate and not very much cocoa butter. If you eat a lot of this type of chocolate, you can get fat.

Most chocolate makers agree: it is best to eat only a few pieces at one time, and often it is good to try the darker chocolate without a lot of fat and sugar. Perhaps this type is a little more expensive, but it can be better for you.

8   Types of chocolate

There are many types of chocolate and each one has a different taste and colour. When people describe chocolate, they sometimes say that it is high in cocoa solids. These cocoa solids give chocolate its special flavour. Chocolate with lots of cocoa solids is usually rich, dark, and more expensive.

Dark chocolate has 35 per cent or more cocoa solids, and it is made with some sugar but usually no milk. There are different types of dark chocolate; if you want to cook with it, often the stronger ones with around 70 per cent cocoa solids are best.

You can even buy special dark chocolate with 99 per cent cocoa solids – it is *very* strong and only real chocolate lovers enjoy eating it. You can make wonderful chocolate cakes with it or perhaps rich chocolate ice cream.

Milk chocolate is lighter in colour and sweeter than dark chocolate. When producers make milk chocolate they take out some of the cocoa solids and put in milk for a smoother flavour. Most cheaper milk chocolate has about 20 per cent cocoa solids but more expensive milk chocolate from Switzerland or France has around 40 per cent.

White chocolate is very different from other types of chocolate – in a lot of countries you cannot even call it 'chocolate'! That's because it is made without cocoa solids and it is mostly cocoa butter, sugar, and milk.

Very clever *chocolatiers* – chocolate makers – can produce beautiful small chocolates. They often use a special type of chocolate for these called *couverture*. Couverture has a lot of cocoa butter in it and you can make it into very thin chocolate.

Over the years chocolatiers have thought of many different types of these wonderful smaller chocolates. For example, in 1912 a Belgian man called Jean Neuhaus invented a new chocolate. He used couverture to produce a thin shell with a hole in the middle. He could then put soft centres inside. These soft centres were made with nuts or soft chocolate. They could also be different flavours like fruit or coffee. Neuhaus called these new

Milk, dark, and white chocolate

Pralines

sweets pralines and they are still made by hand today in many of the three hundred chocolate businesses in Belgium. Good chocolate is very important in Belgium and you can find more than 2,000 chocolate shops in the towns and villages there.

And of course, the French make famous small chocolates, too. In the nineteenth century, chocolatiers mixed chocolate with cream and made small balls from

Truffles

this paste. They then put cocoa powder over these balls and invented the chocolate truffle. Chocolate makers in France still produce truffles by hand today and put them in little boxes. They are often very expensive but they have a wonderful creamy flavour.

In Italy small chocolates with nuts in them are very popular.

In 1865, the famous Italian chocolatier Caffarel invented a new type of sweet – it was made from chocolate and a special nut paste. These small long chocolates were called *giandujas*. Today most Italian chocolate shops sell them but each person makes their giandujas in a secret and special way.

Modern chocolatiers still invent new chocolates, but sometimes these can be very expensive. The Swiss chocolate maker Delafée makes gold pralines which have very small pieces of real gold over them! Of course, it is very special, thin gold and you can easily eat it.

If you are interested in expensive chocolates, there are also the beautiful dark chocolate truffles from the chocolate maker Knipschildt in Connecticut, USA. How much do they cost? Only 250 dollars *each*! They are the most expensive chocolates in the world!

Chocolate with gold

9 Special days and presents

Chocolate is a popular present for birthdays, but in many different places around the world it is important on other special days too.

In Japan and Korea, the most important time for chocolate is Valentine's Day on 14 February. It is a day when people talk and think about love. Women buy chocolate for men or sometimes they make things at home like chocolate balls with the flavour of green tea.

The women usually give two types of presents. Firstly, they buy an expensive present for their 'true love' – a man who is very special to them. Then they buy smaller chocolate presents for the men at their office or place of work. In this way, most men stay happy!

Valentine's Day in Japan

A month later, on 14 March, the men can reply to the women and give them things too. This day is called White Day. Creamy white chocolates in beautiful white boxes are one of the best presents to get on White Day.

In March or April people in some countries give chocolate Easter eggs. The first chocolate eggs were made in France and Germany in the nineteenth century and they soon became popular in many other European countries too.

In Italy today, people often give very large chocolate Easter eggs in beautiful paper. Children usually open their eggs quickly and look for the special surprise inside – perhaps more sweets or something to play with. Adults sometimes find something more expensive. There are stories of gold rings inside chocolate Easter eggs. These rings ask the question, 'Will you marry me?'

Easter eggs

Families in Europe and North America often hide Easter eggs. This has become popular in Brazil too. Parents hide chocolate eggs around the house on the night before Easter. In the morning, the children quickly run around and find them all.

Chocolate skulls for the Day of the Dead

Mexicans have an important holiday later in the year – the Day of the Dead. On 1 and 2 November, men, women, and children remember the lives of their dead family and friends. They usually make a special place in their home with photos of the dead people. They then put things in front of the pictures like flowers, cacao beans, or sometimes *mole*, a special paste made from chocolate. You can buy small chocolate skulls in all the sweet shops too, and Mexican adults often give them to children at this time.

In some European countries people have a holiday on 6 December – it is called Saint Nicholas's Day. Children in places like Germany, Hungary, and Poland often put their shoes near the door on 5 December. If they are good, they will find nuts, fruit or chocolate money from Saint Nicholas inside them next morning.

In the UK parents sometimes give chocolate money to their children on Christmas Day – 25 December. They also put little chocolate sweets on the Christmas trees inside their homes.

All these holidays are very good for chocolate makers. In some countries the factories work for months and months to make the chocolate for these special days. In Japan, for example, chocolate producers sell about half of all their chocolate just before Valentine's Day.

Christmas tree chocolates

10 Cooking with chocolate

People cook with chocolate all over the world, but they often use chocolate in very different ways. Some cooks use chocolate in meals with meat and vegetables. Others make very sweet chocolate cakes with cream on the top.

Some of the oldest and most famous chocolate cakes come from Austria. One of these has an interesting story behind it. In 1832, a sixteen-year-old boy was working in the kitchens of the important leader Prince Metternich. This young cook was called Franz Sacher.

Sachertorte

One day, some very rich visitors came to Metternich's house but the oldest and most important cook suddenly became ill. That night Metternich spoke to Franz. He asked the boy to make something special for his visitors. Franz worked hard and he made a wonderful chocolate cake. The famous Austrian *Sachertorte* was born!

Sachertorte today is a rich, dark chocolate cake with jam in the middle. Real Sachertortes only come from the Austrian towns of Vienna and Salzburg. People often have lots of cream and a strong cup of coffee with a piece of this cake.

You can find very good chocolate cakes in Germany too. Perhaps the most famous one is the Black Forest gateau. This comes from the south-west of Germany and people first began to make it there in the early twentieth century.

Black Forest gateau

A Black Forest gateau is a type of 'sandwich' cake. First, you need to cook three or four thin chocolate cakes. On top of one cake you put cherries and cream, then another cake, and you go on like this until you have one big cake. Of course, you have to put more cherries and lots of cream on the top too!

The French also make interesting chocolate cakes. If you go into French tea shops, you often find long thin cakes with cream inside and chocolate on the top. These chocolate eclairs were first made in France in the nineteenth century and are popular all over the world. Some Americans even celebrate a special eclair day on 22 June every year!

When people talk about cakes and chocolate in countries like Spain, Brazil, and Mexico, they often think

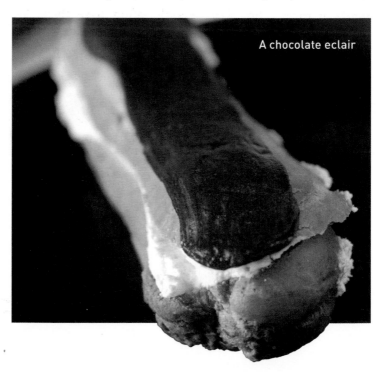

A chocolate eclair

Churros with chocolate

of *churros*. Churros are little cakes and they are usually made without chocolate. People often have these for breakfast with a big cup of hot chocolate. They put the end of the churro into the chocolate and then eat it.

At the end of a meal, Swiss families sometimes have a chocolate fondue. For this fondue, you first need to melt a few bars of chocolate (some people mix in some cream). Next, you pour the chocolate into a large pot. You take pieces of fruit, cake, or sweets, leave these for a second in the warm chocolate and then eat them. It is a good way to finish a meal!

Of course, chocolate is not only in sweet things. There are many different types of the Mexican paste called mole and some of these have dark chocolate in them. Mexicans use mole in their cooking, and they often put it over meat like chicken.

In the US in the 1930s a cook put chocolate chips – very small pieces of chocolate – into some biscuits. These were the first chocolate chip cookies (the American word for biscuits) and they soon became very popular. This is how you make them:

American chocolate chip cookies

Ingredients:
100g butter
100g sugar
1 egg
100g plain flour
25g chocolate chips

1 Mix together the butter and the sugar. Put in the egg and mix again.

2 Then mix in the flour and the chocolate chips to make a paste.

3 Make the paste into a long thin shape with your hands. Put it into a cold place for 30 minutes.

4 Cut thin round pieces off the end of the long shape and put them on a baking tray.

5 Cook these at 180 °C for 10 to 12 minutes until they are a nice gold colour.

6 Leave the cookies until they are cold. They are now ready to eat!

If you *really* like chocolate, you can also put in 25g of cocoa powder with the flour. Then you will have Chocolate chocolate chip cookies!

11 Chocolate places to visit

If you want to find out more about chocolate, you can go to hundreds of special shops, museums, and visitor centres in different countries.

One of the most interesting chocolate museums is in Barcelona, in Catalonia, Spain. You can find some of Barcelona's most famous buildings here, but of course, they are all made of chocolate. You can also learn how to make it. If the wonderful smell makes you hungry, do not worry. You get a good ticket when you arrive – it is a bar of chocolate and you can eat it while you are walking round!

Visitors to Prague in the Czech Republic can also go to an unusual small museum. It has pictures by the artist Vladomir Čech and he made them all in chocolate. At the museum, you can try making a picture yourself. But be careful – it is not easy!

One of the bigger museums is on Jeju-do island in South Korea. It is in a large building

A chocolate painting

which is made of beautiful local stone. You can walk around the three different floors of the museum and learn everything about chocolate. Luckily, you do not only look at the chocolate – before you leave, you can taste a lot of it too.

Cadbury World in Birmingham in the UK is also a favourite place with chocolate lovers. Over 500,000 people travel there every year to find out about the Cadbury story.

The visitor centre is next to their famous factory. You can stand in a corner of the building and watch while people make real Cadbury Dairy Milk. Hundreds of bars go past your eyes every minute – it is very exciting!

Hershey's Chocolate World in the USA is even more popular, with around three million visitors every year. It is a lot more than just a museum because you can visit a special 3D cinema here and go on a ride too. People sit in little cars that move from room to room, and on the journey they learn all about Hershey's chocolate.

A newer place to visit is World Chocolate Wonderland in Beijing. When this was first built, they made a lot of famous Chinese things in chocolate. There was a 12-metre-long Great Wall of China and a Terracotta Army with 560 soldiers! All this used 80 tonnes of the best Belgian chocolate! When World Chocolate Wonderland opened there was also a special fashion show. And what were all the clothes made of? Chocolate, of course.

October is an important time of year for chocolate. If you go to the old town of Perugia in Italy, you can enjoy Eurochocolate. For nine days crowds of visitors walk

A chocolate Terracotta Army

through the narrow old streets here and see chocolate pictures, chocolate cooking, and special chocolate shows. When you get tired at Eurochocolate, you can always sit down and have an Italian ice cream. There is white chocolate, chocolate chip, dark chocolate . . . sometimes it is difficult to decide. And at the end of the day, you can go back to your hotel. What is it called? The Chocohotel. This hotel has a great sweet shop and everything on the restaurant menu has chocolate in it.

A chocolate hat

12 Changing chocolate

Chocolate has a long story, from the time of the Olmecs three thousand years ago until today. Over the years it has changed a lot. It started as a very strong drink which people made by hand. But now it is very different – we have rich smooth chocolate bars from big modern factories.

And chocolate is still changing. Every year, there are new chocolate flavours. In Japan, for example, you can now buy chocolate bars with some very unusual flavours. Do you like the sound of apple or sweet potato flavour? Or perhaps green tea or blood orange?

Chocolate producers sell more chocolate every year and in some countries it has become important in everyday life. The producers say that when times are hard, people stop buying expensive cars and going out – but they do not stop buying chocolate!

Until now, people have not eaten much chocolate in some Asian countries like India and China. But tastes are now starting to change. In China, young men and women are becoming interested in sweeter food from Europe and America. The World Chocolate Wonderland in Beijing is important for some producers because it can help to sell chocolate in China.

Of course, when people eat more chocolate, the cacao tree plantations need to grow more and more cacao beans. But this leaves us with a lot of questions. What about the smaller farmers? Will they ever get more money for their beans? Will their workers get fair pay? Will there still be stories of child workers on plantations? And how will bigger plantations change the shape of the rainforest in some places?

But one thing is sure: chocolate has been with us for thousands of years, and people all over the world love its truly wonderful taste. Chocolate is big business and it is here to stay.

GLOSSARY

baking tray a small sheet of metal used for baking food on
bar a piece of something with straight sides
become to begin to be something
biscuit (US **cookie**) a small, flat, sweet, dry cake
bubble a ball of air in a liquid
caffeine something found in coffee that makes you feel
    more awake
cake a sweet food made from flour, eggs, sugar and butter
century a time of one hundred years
chemical something solid or liquid that is made by chemistry
cherry a small, soft, round, red or black fruit
cream the thick yellow-white liquid on the top of milk
disease an illness
Easter a Christian festival on a Sunday in March or April
explore to travel around a new place to learn about it
fair treating everybody equally or in the right way
farmer a person who keeps animals or grows plants for food
fat (*n & adj*) something solid or liquid that comes from animals
    or plants; with a large round body
flavour a special type of taste in food
force to make somebody do something that they do not want
    to do
god a spirit that people believe has power over them and nature
grind (past tense **ground**) to break something into very small
    pieces or powder
grow (of a plant) to live somewhere; to plant something in the
    ground and look after it
ice cream a very cold sweet food made from milk
ingredient one of the things that you put in when you make
    something to eat
invent to make something for the first time
jam sweet food made from fruit and sugar
king the most important man in a country

local belonging to a particular place

machine a thing with moving parts that is made to do a job

melt to become liquid after becoming warmer

mix to put different things together to make something new

museum a building where people can look at old or interesting
things

nut a small hard fruit with a hard shell that grows on a tree

paste a soft wet mixture of powder and liquid

plain flour flour that has no baking powder (used to make cakes
high and light) in it

plantation a big piece of land where a lot of trees or plants grow,
like cacao trees or bananas

pot a deep round container for putting food in

pour to make liquid go out of or into something

powder something dry that is made of a lot of very small pieces

prince (princess) a man (woman) in a royal family

produce to make something

pulp the soft part inside some fruit

rainforest a forest in a hot part of the world where there is a lot
of rain

rule (of a king or queen) to control a country

scientific of or about science

shape the form of the outside of something

shell the hard outside part of a nut

skull the bones in the head of a person

slave a person who must work for another person for no money

smooth very flat, with no big pieces in it

spice a small part of a plant that you put in food to make it
taste good

sugar a sweet white or brown substance that you put in food

tonne a thousand kilograms

trade to buy and sell things; (*n*) **trader**

type a group of things that are the same in some way

welcome (*v & adj*) to show a visitor that you are happy to
see them

ACTIVITIES

Before Reading

1 What do you know about chocolate? Circle *a*, *b* or *c*.

1 Where do people grow the most cacao beans?
a) Ivory Coast   b) Indonesia   c) Brazil

2 Who eats the most chocolate in the world?
a) The Americans   b) The Italians   c) The Swiss

3 When was the first chocolate bar made?
a) 1847   b) 1875   c) 1912

4 Who was the most famous American chocolate producer?
a) John Cadbury   b) Milton Hershey   c) J. S. Fry

5 Where were the first chocolate eclairs made?
a) Spain   b) Switzerland   c) France

6 When do shops in Japan sell the most chocolate?
a) Christmas   b) Valentine's Day   c) New Year

2 Read the text. Circle the correct words.

People first tasted chocolate long ago in *Peru* / *Mexico*. In the beginning people made *drinks* / *sweets* with the cacao beans and on important days they gave these to their *gods* / *kings*. They had very beautiful *plates* / *cups* for their chocolate and we still have some of these today.

Chocolate first came to Europe with the *French* / *Spanish* in the *sixteenth* / *seventeenth* century and people started to put *sugar* / *cheese* in it. At this time, *poor* / *rich* men and women went to small *gardens* / *restaurants* to have chocolate and meet friends.

ACTIVITIES

While Reading

Read Chapter 1. Then rewrite these untrue sentences with the correct information.

1 There are over a thousand flavours in chocolate.
2 Cacao trees first came from the rainforests of South Africa.
3 You can find cacao trees in about ten countries.
4 The very large fruits of the cacao tree are called beans.
5 Cacao trees need cool weather to grow well.
6 Mexican people eat 10.2 kilograms of chocolate a year.
7 The actor Johnny Depp is in three films about chocolate.
8 A Brazilian woman wrote *Like Water for Chocolate*.

Read Chapters 2 and 3. Then fill in the gaps with these names.

Anne of Austria, the Aztecs, the conquistadors, Hernán Cortés, the King of Spain, the Maya, Moctezuma the Second, Samuel Pepys

1 _____ made the first chocolate drink from cacao beans.
2 _____ used cacao beans as money.
3 _____ drank fifty cups of chocolate every day.
4 _____ were looking for silver but found cacao beans.
5 _____ learned about chocolate in a letter from Cortés.
6 _____ fought against Moctezuma with a big army.
7 _____ brought cacao beans to France.
8 _____ wrote about chocolate in a famous diary.

Read Chapter 4. Choose the best question word for these questions, and then answer them.

What / When / Where / Who / Why

1 . . . did Van Houten want to invent a new machine?
2 . . . was the name of Van Houten's machine?
3 . . . made the first chocolate bar?
4 . . . in the UK was this first bar made?
5 . . . invented milk chocolate?
6 . . . did Henri Nestlé invent condensed milk?
7 . . . did Rodolphe Lindt's conching machine do?
8 . . . did Cadbury, Fry and Hershey do to help their workers?

Read Chapter 5. People do these things to make chocolate. Put them in the correct order.

1 The factory workers first cook the beans in a large machine.
2 The plantation workers take the pods from the cacao tree and cut them open.
3 They put the chocolate in the conching machine.
4 They dry the beans in the sun.
5 They make the chocolate very hot then cold, and put it in special boxes to become hard.
6 The brokers buy the beans from the farmers and sell them to chocolate factories.
7 They put the beans under banana leaves.
8 Then they put the beans through three machines.

Read Chapters 6 and 7. Are these sentences true (T) or false (F)? Rewrite the false ones with the correct information.

1 At first, the conquistadors only used African slaves.
2 There are stories today about slaves on African plantations.
3 Farmers always get a lot of money for their cacao beans.
4 Fairtrade began in 1988 to help farmers.
5 A Russian man found theobromine in cacao beans in 1841.
6 Theobromine can be good for animals like cats and dogs.
7 Dark chocolate can be better for you than milk chocolate.

Read Chapters 8 and 9. Then match these halves of sentences.

1 Dark chocolate . . .
2 *Giandujas* . . .
3 Knipschildt truffles . . .
4 Green tea flavour chocolate balls . . .
5 Easter eggs . . .
6 *Mole* . . .
7 Chocolate money . . .

a are made from chocolate and a nut paste.
b always has 35 per cent or more cocoa solids in it.
c is a paste made from chocolate. You can find it in Mexico.
d were first made in Germany and France.
e are made by Japanese women for Valentine's Day.
f are the most expensive chocolates in the world.
g is a present for some children in December.

Read Chapter 10, then fill in the gaps with these words.

1832, 1930s, cherries, chocolate, churros, coffee, cookies, cream, France, fondue, Germany, melt

One very famous _____ cake is the Sachertorte from Austria. It was first made in _____ by a sixteen-year-old boy. People often drink _____ with it.

    In _____, there is the Black Forest gateau. People put _____ and _____ in the middle and on the top.

    In tea shops in _____ you can find chocolate eclairs and in Spain people have _____ with their hot chocolate.

    Swiss families like to _____ chocolate to make a hot _____. They put pieces of fruit in it and then eat them.

    And of course, there are chocolate biscuits. An American cook in the early _____ cut up small pieces of chocolate and gave the world the first chocolate chip _____.

Read Chapters 11 and 12, then answer these questions.

1 What can you do at the chocolate museum in Prague?
2 What is the chocolate museum in South Korea made of?
3 How many visitors go to Cadbury World every year?
4 How do people travel around Hershey's Chocolate World?
5 What famous things were at World Chocolate Wonderland?
6 Where can you stay when you visit Eurochocolate?
7 What unusual flavour chocolate bars can you buy in Japan?
8 What do people stop buying when times are hard?
9 Where haven't people eaten much chocolate until now?

ACTIVITIES

After Reading

1 **Complete the crossword.**

Across:

1 Part of a plant that makes food taste nice. *fruit*

5 J. S. Fry made chocolate into this. *bar*

7 To make something. *produce ?? place??*

10 The Olmecs found cacao trees here.

12 To buy and sell things like cacao beans or coffee. *trade*

Down:

2 Something dry that is made of lots of small pieces. *powder*

3 Sachertorte is a famous type of this. *cake*

4 A ball of air in a liquid. *bubble*

6 A small, hard fruit with a shell. *nut*

7 To make liquid go out of or into something. *pour*

8 If chocolate becomes hot, it does this. *melts*

9 To put two things together, like milk and chocolate. *mix*

11 Cocoa butter is a type of this. *fat*

2 Complete these two letters using the words below.

cake, chocolatl, city, cook, jam, fifty, good, ill, millions,
money, news, rainforest, ruler, Sachertorte, visitors,
welcomed, worked

Dear King Charles

There are so many things to tell you about here in the Aztec _city_ of
Tenochtitlán. When I first arrived, their great _ruler_ Moctezuma _welcomed_
me with a wonderful drink called _chocolatl_

The Aztecs always have this drink in beautiful small cups. It makes you
feel very _good_ and people say that Moctezuma drinks _fifty_ cups of it
every day.

It is made from the beans of a tree in the _rainforest_. These beans are
important to the Aztecs and they use them as both food and _money_
Moctezuma has a bank with _millions_ of beans in it!

I think these beans could be very useful to us. I will try to learn all about
them and tell you more in my next letter.

Yours
Hernán Cortés

Dear Mother

I have some very exciting _____ for you! Yesterday the most important
_____ in our kitchen suddenly became very _____, so Prince
Metternich asked ME to make something special for the _____ to this
house!

I thought a lot and I _____ hard all night. In the end, I made a rich
chocolate _____ with some _____ in the middle. Everybody loved it
and Prince Metternich says he wants to call it _____ after me!

I will make it for you the next time I see you.

Love

Franz

3 Perhaps this is what some of the people in the book are thinking. Who are they? What is happening?

1 'That Spanish soldier is a friendly man. He's very interested in our special drink here. I must tell him more about it.'

2 'Some people like hot chocolate but not me. I hate the pieces of shell in it *and* the fat on top! How can I make it better?'

3 'This chocolate with cheese in it tastes terrible! Now, what other things can I mix with chocolate?'

Choose a famous person from the book. Give a talk about them to your class. Websites like: allthingschocolate.co.uk or en.wikipedia.org can help you to find more information.

4 Do you agree or disagree with these sentences? Why?

1 People in western countries eat too much chocolate now.

2 It is fine for children to eat chocolate sometimes.

3 Chocolate needs to be a lot more expensive. Then the workers on the plantations can get more money.

4 People must stop selling chocolate that is not Fairtrade chocolate.

5 Find a chocolate recipe that you like (websites like bbc. co.uk/food/recipes or allrecipes.co.uk/recipe can help you). Make a poster about your recipe with:

• a list of the ingredients;
• the instructions for making the recipe;
• a photo or picture of what it looks like.

Make your recipe. Bring it to class for everybody to taste!

ABOUT THE AUTHOR

Janet Hardy-Gould is an experienced teacher, writer, and teacher trainer. She is married with two children, and lives in the ancient town of Lewes in the south of England. In her free time, she likes walking across the beautiful hills near her town and meeting friends in cafés for tea and cakes.

She has worked extensively on activities and support materials for OUP readers, notably for the Dominoes series and the Oxford Bookworms Library, and has published titles in both series. Her Bookworms titles are *King Arthur* (Human Interest), *Henry VIII and his Six Wives* (True Stories), *Deserts* (Factfiles) and *Marco Polo and the Silk Road* (Factfiles). For Dominoes, she has written *The Great Fire of London, Mulan, Sinbad, Hercules, Sherlock Holmes: The Emerald Crown*, and *The Travels of Ibn Battuta*.

From an early age, Janet has been very keen on all kinds of chocolate, and she particularly enjoys French chocolate truffles. She has a lot of chocolate cookery books too. Her favourite recipe is Heavenly Pie – a wonderful chocolate tart with cream on the top.

OXFORD BOOKWORMS LIBRARY

Classics • Crime & Mystery • Factfiles • Fantasy & Horror
Human Interest • Playscripts • Thriller & Adventure
True Stories • World Stories

The OXFORD BOOKWORMS LIBRARY provides enjoyable reading in English, with a wide range of classic and modern fiction, non-fiction, and plays. It includes original and adapted texts in seven carefully graded language stages, which take learners from beginner to advanced level. An overview is given on the next pages.

All Stage 1 titles are available as audio recordings, as well as over eighty other titles from Starter to Stage 6. All Starters and many titles at Stages 1 to 4 are specially recommended for younger learners. Every Bookworm is illustrated, and Starters and Factfiles have full-colour illustrations.

The OXFORD BOOKWORMS LIBRARY also offers extensive support. Each book contains an introduction to the story, notes about the author, a glossary, and activities. Additional resources include tests and worksheets, and answers for these and for the activities in the books. There is advice on running a class library, using audio recordings, and the many ways of using Oxford Bookworms in reading programmes. Resource materials are available on the website <www.oup.com/elt/bookworms>.

The *Oxford Bookworms Collection* is a series for advanced learners. It consists of volumes of short stories by well-known authors, both classic and modern. Texts are not abridged or adapted in any way, but carefully selected to be accessible to the advanced student.

You can find details and a full list of titles in the *Oxford Bookworms Library Catalogue* and *Oxford English Language Teaching Catalogues*, and on the website <www.oup.com/elt/bookworms>.

THE OXFORD BOOKWORMS LIBRARY
GRADING AND SAMPLE EXTRACTS

STARTER • 250 HEADWORDS

present simple – present continuous – imperative –
can/cannot, must – *going to* (future) – simple gerunds …

Her phone is ringing – but where is it?

Sally gets out of bed and looks in her bag. No phone. She looks under the bed. No phone. Then she looks behind the door. There is her phone. Sally picks up her phone and answers it. *Sally's Phone*

STAGE 1 • 400 HEADWORDS

… past simple – coordination with *and, but, or* –
subordination with *before, after, when, because, so* …

I knew him in Persia. He was a famous builder and I worked with him there. For a time I was his friend, but not for long. When he came to Paris, I came after him – I wanted to watch him. He was a very clever, very dangerous man. *The Phantom of the Opera*

STAGE 2 • 700 HEADWORDS

… present perfect – *will* (future) – *(don't) have to, must not, could* –
comparison of adjectives – simple *if* clauses – past continuous –
tag questions – *ask/tell* + infinitive …

While I was writing these words in my diary, I decided what to do. I must try to escape. I shall try to get down the wall outside. The window is high above the ground, but I have to try. I shall take some of the gold with me – if I escape, perhaps it will be helpful later. *Dracula*

STAGE 3 • 1000 HEADWORDS

... should, may – present perfect continuous – *used to* – past perfect
– causative – relative clauses – indirect statements ...

Of course, it was most important that no one should see
Colin, Mary, or Dickon entering the secret garden. So Colin
gave orders to the gardeners that they must all keep away
from that part of the garden in future. *The Secret Garden*

STAGE 4 • 1400 HEADWORDS

... past perfect continuous – passive (simple forms) –
would conditional clauses – indirect questions –
relatives with *where/when* – gerunds after prepositions/phrases ...

I was glad. Now Hyde could not show his face to the world
again. If he did, every honest man in London would be proud
to report him to the police. *Dr Jekyll and Mr Hyde*

STAGE 5 • 1800 HEADWORDS

... future continuous – future perfect –
passive (modals, continuous forms) –
would have conditional clauses – modals + perfect infinitive ...

If he had spoken Estella's name, I would have hit him. I was so
angry with him, and so depressed about my future, that I could
not eat the breakfast. Instead I went straight to the old house.
Great Expectations

STAGE 6 • 2500 HEADWORDS

... passive (infinitives, gerunds) – advanced modal meanings –
clauses of concession, condition

When I stepped up to the piano, I was confident. It was as if I
knew that the prodigy side of me really did exist. And when I
started to play, I was so caught up in how lovely I looked that
I didn't worry how I would sound. *The Joy Luck Club*

BOOKWORMS · FACTFILES · STAGE 2

Marco Polo and the Silk Road

JANET HARDY-GOULD

For a child in the great city of Venice in the thirteenth century, there could be nothing better than the stories of sailors. There were stories of strange animals, wonderful cities, sweet spices, and terrible wild deserts where a traveller could die. One young boy listened, waited, and dreamed. Perhaps one day his father and uncle would return. Perhaps he too could travel with them to great markets in faraway places. For young Marco Polo, later the greatest traveller of his time, a dangerous, exciting world was waiting . . .

BOOKWORMS · FACTFILES · STAGE 2

Seasons and Celebrations

JACKIE MAGUIRE

In English-speaking countries around the world people celebrate Easter, Valentine's Day, Christmas, and other special days. Some celebrations are new, others, like the summer solstice, go back thousands of years.

What happens on these special days? Why is there a special day for eating pancakes? Who is the 'guy' that children take onto the streets in November? And where do many people like to spend the shortest night of the year in England?

Come on a journey through a year of celebrations, from New Year's Eve to Christmas.